Rebuilding the Temple

Rebuilding the Temple

Preparing for the Lord's Return

Enoch Lavender

TESTIMONIALS

"Many Christians understand that one day the Jewish temple will be rebuilt in Jerusalem - however few have kept up to date with the current movement in Israel to accomplish this.

Enoch Lavender, in his well researched and written book brings together the most recent real world events and actions that are examined in the light of Bible prophecy. Written in bite-sized bits so that this scholarly subject can be easily understood and digested for the scholar and lay person alike."

Kade Hawkins
Founder and CEO of Prophecy News Watch

"*Rebuilding the Temple* is not just a great read—it's an important read. The bubbling tensions of the Middle-East, which spill onto our Western streets, is ultimately about the piece of real-estate God chose for His habitation!

Re-building the Temple is not just informative; it is a challenge to the Church. Enoch Lavender skillfully connects the dots of Bible prophecy, current events, and End-time expectations and preparations of Jews, Muslims and Christians alike. The Lord will "suddenly" come to His temple. "He is coming", says the Lord of Hosts. (Mal 3:1)"

Ruth Webb B. Mus Ed.
Tabernacle of David (Bendigo)

TESTIMONIALS

> *"My eyes will be open and My ears attentive to prayer made in this place.*
> *For now I have chosen and sanctified this house,*
> *that My name may be there forever;*
> *and My eyes and My heart will be there perpetually.'*
> (2 Chron 7:12-16)

To my Mum who patiently assisted in proof reading,
To all who have invested spiritually in my life,
And ultimately to Jesus, my Saviour to whom I owe everything.

Copyright © 2018, 2022 by Enoch Lavender

All rights reserved. No part of this book may be reproduced in any manner whatsoever without written permission except in the case of brief quotations embodied in critical articles and reviews.

Unless otherwise indicated, Scripture taken from the New King James Version. Copyright © 1982 by Thomas Nelson, Inc. Used by permission. All rights reserved.

The internet addresses in this publication are accurate at the time of publication. They are provided as a resource.

Revised 2018 version, first printing, 2022

CONTENTS

DEDICATION vii

The Situation on the Ground

1 | Facing East 2

2 | Israel and the Temple 5

3 | The Temple Mount is in Our Hands 11

4 | The Stunning Rise of Yehudah Glick 20

Preparing for the Temple

5 | Temple Vessels and the Priesthood 28

6 | Preparing the Way (literally) 37

The Temple in Prophecy

7 | Daniel's 70 Weeks 44

8 | Hanukkah and the Abomination of Desolation 48

CONTENTS

9 | The Architect – Cyrus or the AntiChrist? 59

10 | Islam and the Temple 65

Christians and the Temple

11 | Can Christians Support the Rebuilding of the Temple? 72

12 | A Theological Earthquake 78

APPENDIXES	83
THE CITY OF DAVID THEORY	85
THE MILLENIUM AND BEYOND	93
ENTERING THE HOLY OF HOLIES	101
SELECTED BIBLIOGRAPHY	105
ABOUT THE AUTHOR	106

The Situation on the Ground

1

Facing East

Looking at any Biblical map of Jerusalem you will notice the Temple of God dominating the city. It was a magnificent structure which would truly have been the pride of the city and represented nothing less than God Himself dwelling among mankind.

Yet, looking more closely at the map, you will notice something rather puzzling – the Temple seems to be facing away from the city of Jerusalem. This was true for King Solomon's Temple, which was built to the north of the ancient citadel and faced away to the east. It was also true for the Second Temple in Jesus' day. By then, the City of Jerusalem had grown in size, yet it's houses, streets and bustling markets were all located either to the west or the south of the Temple – with the Temple standing seemingly with its back facing away from the city and towards the east.

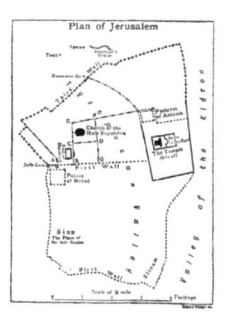

Jerusalem Map
(public domain)

The Temple was built after divine instruction given to King David, yet I'm sure many would have questioned this rather odd design. Shouldn't the Temple be facing the people of Jerusalem?

In Scripture, God often commanded His people to do something a certain way – and only later explained why. In the case of the Temple's odd direction, it is not until we get to the prophecies of Ezekiel that we finally get some light on this unusual design.

Ezekiel chapters 8 to 11 foretell the departure of the glory of God from the Temple – detailing how it would leave the Temple and head east to the Mount of Olives and then ascend to the heavens. It is interesting to note that after His resurrection, Jesus also ascended from the very same site on the Mount of Olives, east of Jerusalem.

Ezekiel 43-44 portrays God's glory returning the same way it left – from the Mount of Olives to enter Jerusalem and the Temple from the east. This prophecy seems to speak of Jesus' return, as we know from other Scriptures that He will one day return to the Mount of Olives and enter Jerusalem from the East (Is. 63:1, Acts 1:11). Being aware of these messianic prophecies, Islamic leaders have sealed shut the Eastern Gate to the Temple Mount with a brick wall – but as you and I know, our Messiah has no problem going through brick walls!

Coming back to the direction of the Temple, it can be seen that it was not built facing eastward for the sake of the people, or for the sake of the many travelling pilgrims to the city. The Temple was built this way to fulfil its ultimate purpose– which is to welcome the King of Glory to His rightful place. This is the top priority for the Temple, and by this pattern it was built.

As this book explores the prospect of the Temple being rebuilt in our days, remember that while the Temple in itself is magnificent and fascinating, its primary purpose is to point us to the King of Glory who will one day return to dwell among His people in Jerusalem.

May the developments concerning the Temple's rebuilding in our days inspire us all to be ready for that great day when our Lord will return!

2

Israel and the Temple

Returning to Rebuild

At Mt Sinai, God gave Israel a mandate to build Him a 'sanctuary' that He might dwell among them (Ex. 25:8, Deut. 12:5-12). As they entered the land of Israel, this mandate led to the construction of the magnificent First Temple under King Solomon.

After the destruction of the Temple and the subsequent Jewish exile to Babylon, God again brought His people back to the land He had chosen. This time they arrived with support from King Cyrus to rebuild God's house (Ezra 1:2) – resulting in the Second Temple being built through the perseverance of leaders like Ezra, Zerubbabel and Nehemiah.

This temple stood for 600 years until the Roman destruction in 70 AD. In an effort to destroy the Jewish nation once and for all, Rome decreed the Jews into exile. Over the coming centuries, the Jewish people were gradually scattered to the four corners of the globe. However, the God of the Bible had not forgotten His people. The God of Israel promised to one day bring His people back even if they were exiled to the '*farthest parts under heaven*', affirming that He would indeed bring them back '*to the land which your fathers possessed*' (Deut 30:4).

In one of the greatest miracles in our modern times, millions of Jewish people have returned to the Land of Israel as envisioned by Isaiah – from the north, south, east and west (Is 43:6). Just like in Bible days, regathered Israel has been victorious against all odds in war after war – and her very existence after the holocaust is truly a miracle and a testimony to God's power.

Haggai's Message

Given the miracle of Israel's existence, given her regathering again to her homeland from the four corners of the world and given the Torah commandments, why then hasn't Israel built the temple yet? Surely, if Haggai the prophet was alive today, wouldn't he scald Israel again saying: "*How long will you dwell in paneled houses while this Temple lies in ruins?*" (Hag. 1:4)

In this chapter we will see several reasons why Israel has not built the Temple – while in the following chapters we will see how recent developments are none-the-less pushing Israel towards the Third Temple.

Jewish Opposition

It might surprise Christians to learn that a majority of religious Jews oppose any efforts to rebuild the Temple today.

A few years ago, I attended a lecture by a Jewish Zionist leader. During the Q&A after the lecture, a keen Christian took note of the man's obvious faith in the God of Israel and asked him about his thoughts on rebuilding the Temple. His response – which took several of us Christians by surprise - was to explain that he was not at all interested in the rebuilding of the Temple. He went on to explain how he viewed the sacrificial system as something quaint and irrelevant nowadays and that he was glad to leave it in the dustbin of history.

Of the Orthodox Jews who believe the Temple should be rebuilt, most hold that it can only be rebuilt by the Messiah in the Messianic era.

How does this line up with the many Torah commandments that are contingent on the existence of the Temple? Well, after the destruction of the Second Temple, mainstream Judaism has adapted itself to a religion no longer dependent upon sacrifices. Instead modern Rabbinic Judaism emphasizes good works and Torah observance as a path to right standing with God.

While the site of the ancient Temple remains revered across the spectrum of Judaism, the concept of rebuilding the Temple has been relegated to the dreams of a small minority within the community.

Fears of an International Backlash

Apart from a lack of religiously motivated enthusiasm to rebuild the Temple, another dampening factor is the very real fear that any such moves would trigger off an immediate World War III. Having seen the firestorm surrounding President Trump's Jerusalem embassy decision, one can only imagine what kind of reaction would be triggered by a decision to re-build the Temple!

The Temple Mount is today occupied by the third holiest site in Islam, namely the Al Aqsa Mosque and the picturesque Dome of the Rock. In addition, many Muslims see the entire site as one gigantic mosque – meaning that any Jewish presence or prayers anywhere on the site is in itself seen as a violation of the sanctity of the site.

Highlighting the level of Islamic concern for this site, the Organisation of Islamic Co-Operation was founded in 1969 with the specific goal of protecting the Al-Aqsa mosque. Today this influential organisation boasts 56 member states and is the second largest intergovernmental organisation in the world after the UN.

With such a huge body of nations dead-set against any strengthened Jewish presence on the Temple Mount, and the desire to rebuild the Temple being a fringe view within Judaism, Temple Mount activists have been seen by many Israelis as irresponsible trouble makers who need to be kept in check to avoid a major international conflict.

OIC Member States. Russia is an observer
M.WongM
(https://commons.wikimedia.org/wiki/File:OIC_vector_map.svg), „OIC vector map", https://creativecommons.org/licenses/by-sa/3.0/legalcode

Will there be a Third Temple?

Despite the clear Torah mandate, the circumstances truly make it unlikely for the Temple to be rebuilt any time soon. In fact, successive Israeli governments of all political persuasions have firmly and repeatedly committed themselves to maintaining the 'status quo' on the Temple Mount to avoid fermenting trouble.

Regardless of these seemingly impossible circumstances, both the Old and New Testaments predict the presence of an End Time temple. In the New Testament, Jesus (Mt. 24:15) and Paul both (2 Thes. 2:3-4) foretell an End Time defilement of the Temple. Although some may argue that this refers to a 'spiritual temple' (i.e. the church), these predictions would have been understood by their original listeners as referring to the literal building itself. Daniel's Old Testament prophecy concerning the daily sacrifices being taken away is also best understood to refer to a literal Temple.

The building of the Third Temple in our day may seem impossible, but it also looked impossible for the impoverished exiles returning to build the Second Temple in the days of Zerubbabel. With mounting opposition from the nations around and countless delays, Zechariah the prophet spoke the timeless words *'not by might, nor by power, but by My Spirit says the Lord'* (Zec 4:6). Against all odds, God's Spirit indeed strengthened the hands of the builders and enabled the construction of the Second Temple. For the Third Temple to be built, it will likewise have to be through a supernatural move of God to open the doors, remove opposition and make the impossible possible.

As you read through this book, you will see the beginning of these ancient prophecies concerning the Temple coming to pass in our Age. As you read about the unlikely and miraculous events bringing Israel closer towards the rebuilding of the Temple, know that we are truly getting close to the Lord's return.

In the next chapter, we are going to look at the birthing of the modern day Temple Movement, and will see how Israel's miraculous

6 Day War set in motion prophetic developments that are still reverberating across the Middle East today.

3

The Temple Mount is in Our Hands

To understand the modern Temple movement and several of its key players, we first have to go back to the 6 Day War of 1967.

The first half of 1967 were dark days for Israel. Under the leadership of Egyptian strongman Nasser, the Arab world were actively mobilizing their armies on Israel's borders while openly calling for Israel's complete annihilation.

Israel meanwhile seemed to be faltering under the timid and non-charismatic leadership of Prime Minister Levi Eshkol. Seeking to re-assure the increasingly concerned nation, Prime Minister Levi held a live radio broadcast. The broadcast ended up having the opposite effect, as Levi stuttered, hesitated, coughed and stumbled his way through the live speech.

In the looming conflict, the odds were stacked against Israel as she faced Arab armies boasting twice as many men, five times as many tanks (5000 vs 1000) and four times more air craft (900 vs

196). Under intense pressure to find a solution and blamed by some for bringing Israel to the very brink of destruction, Israel's Army Chief of Staff Yitzhak Rabin suffered a nervous breakdown and stepped down temporarily.

During these dark days, public parks in Jerusalem and Tel Aviv were designated for mass graves – in anticipation of a minimum of 20'000 casualties in the impending onslaught.

Israel Strikes

In response to the building tension and in a desperate bid to get the upper hand, Israel launched a surprise all out aerial assault on Egypt in the morning of June 5th. Leaving only a handful of aircraft behind, it was an all or nothing assault which placed the nation's future on the line. The element of surprise was crucial, and thankfully for Israel, Egyptian radar failed to pick up the incoming aircraft.

Jordanian radar however did spot the swarm of planes and sent a coded emergency alert to the Egyptians. While the alert was received, the Egyptian military staff were unable to decode the warning as they had recently changed their encoding frequencies and were unable to read messages using the old code.

The air strike turned out to be a stunning success, decimating the Egyptian air force on the tarmac while the Egyptian pilots were having breakfast - dramatically altering the course of the war.

The Egyptian authorities meanwhile did not want to admit their humiliating losses and began broadcasting fictional reports of great victories against Israel. Furthermore, they encouraged Jordan and Syria to enter the 'victorious' war against Israel. Without the

Egyptian air-power, Jordan's attack on Israel was doomed as her troops were systematically routed by the Israelis in the following days until the war ended on the 6th day of the conflict.[1]

Messianic Author Joel Rosenberg sums up the miraculous nature of the war: "In six days, the Jewish people defended themselves, destroyed their enemies, tripled their land; recaptured control of Jerusalem for the first time in 2,000 years and on the seventh day they rested."[2]

It was truly a miraculous and unexpected turn around – but also an event of huge prophetic implications as Jerusalem was back under Jewish control for the first time in over 1900 years.

The Temple Mount and the 6 Day War

On June 6th 1967, the now famous words of Paratroopers Brigade Commander Motti Gur resounded across the nation of Israel: 'The Temple Mount is in our hands'.

Rugged and war-weary Israeli soldiers who had been engaged in a battle for the very survival of the Jewish state, found themselves unexpectedly conquering the Old City of Jerusalem. The soldiers streamed to the Western Wall towards which the Jewish people had prayed ever since the destruction of the Temple in 70 A.D. Even secular Israeli soldiers who had never prayed a prayer in their lives were seen openly weeping and asking their fellow soldiers how to pray.

Meanwhile, dramatic encounters were taking place that day on the Temple Mount itself – encounters which would forever change lives and would lay the foundation for the modern-day movement to rebuild the Temple.

Among the Israeli soldiers roaming the Temple Mount was Paratrooper Ezra Orni. With permission from his commander, Ezra dramatically hoisted the Israeli flag over the famed Dome of the Rock. Ezra's commander Motti Gur meanwhile held a brigade roll call for his paratroopers on the Temple Mount Plaza itself.

Addressing his men on the Temple Mount with the backdrop of the Israeli flag adorning the Islamic Shrine, Motti spoke of the heroes of Israel's past including the Maccabees who liberated Jerusalem and rededicated the Temple in 164BC. Motti's men had a lot in common with the Maccabees and had overcome similar overwhelming odds to return to Israel's holiest sites. The paratroopers must have felt a sense of destiny about returning to Judaism's most sacred ground, and Motti's words about the ancient battles for the Temple would have resonated deeply. Was Motti's brigade destined to be part of a new generation of heroic Maccabees – returning the Jewish people to the Temple Mount?

Separately a group of Israeli soldiers entered the Dome of the Rock itself, quickly forming a 'minyan' (group of ten men required for Jewish worship) and spent time in prayer on this uniquely holy site.

IDF chief chaplain, Rabbi Shlomo Goren did not exactly attempt to restrain the troops' religious excitement. Having sounded the shofar and prayed at the Western Wall, the excited and fiery Rabbi ascended the Temple Mount and entered the Dome of the Rock itself. There Rabbi Goren – armed with his Torah Scroll - proceeded to encircle the Foundation Stone. This is the very stone upon which the Ark of the Covenant is believed to have rested in the Holy of Holies.

Upon exiting, Rabbi Goren excitedly approached IDF commander Uzi Narkiss. "In preparation for the imminent Messianic era", he suggested, "the IDF should utilize its explosives on hand to demolish the mosques on the Temple Mount".[3]

A Stunning Disappointment

Rabbi Goren was in for a stunning disappointment - IDF commander Narkiss not only ignored Goren's request – but according to some reports even threatened Goren with prison if he kept on with this idea.

Meanwhile, Israel Defence Minister Moshe Dayan spotted the Israeli flag adorning the Dome of the Rock and immediately ordered its removal. The Israeli government had long been concerned that capturing Jerusalem might spark an international backlash from the powerful Christian, Catholic and Islamic communities. The deeply secular Moshe Dayan therefore acted quickly to return control of all religious sites in Jerusalem to their respective religious leaders – and proceeded to also hand control of the Temple Mount back to the Islamic world represented by the Islamic Waqf.

It all happened so quickly – and the golden moment of opportunity to begin rebuilding the Temple was gone as suddenly as it had appeared.

The Birthing of the Temple Movement

Although Rabbi Goren's dreams were dashed, the seeds of Israel's Temple Mount Movement were sown deeply into the lives of two young men that very day.

Born into a family with a heritage of longing for the rebuilding of the Temple, Gershon Salomon was grievously wounded in battle against the Syrians. He experienced a miraculous deliverance from his would-be Syrian executioners and felt in that moment God calling him to dedicate his life to the rebuilding of the Temple. As Israel conquered the Temple Mount in 67, Gershon – still on crutches – joined his fellow Israeli soldiers on the sacred grounds. What he witnessed that day would change his life forever.

As Gerson and his fellow soldiers toured the Temple Mount, they encountered a neatly dressed Jordanian guide. Addressing them in English, the guide proceeded to give the Israelis a tour of the site, explaining where the Temple, the menorah and the altar originally stood. When asked by the group of soldiers why he was showing them all this, the Jordanian guide reportedly answered "we have a tradition from our fathers [and] they from their fathers that one day the Jews would wage a war and conquer this mountain and rebuild the Holy Temple"[4]. Addressing the incredulous Israelis, the guide went even further saying, "I assume that you're starting tomorrow".

Gershon further relates that the tour guide seemed to suddenly disappear, and the whole experience appeared so miraculous that he and other soldiers assumed the guide must have been an Angel. Facing towards the Holy of Holies, Gershon solemnly pledged that day to work ceaselessly for the re-building of the Temple.

While Gershon was bitterly disappointed with Dayan's decision to hand back the Temple Mount to Islamic control, Gershon remained faithful to his word and established the 'Temple Mount Faithful' organisation. Gershon has since that time advocated tirelessly for the rebuilding of the Temple – admonishing the Israeli nation with words from Haggai the prophet *"Is it time for you, yourselves, to dwell in your well-timbered houses, while this house lies in ruins?" (Hag. 1:2)*

Another young man whose life was changed that day was Paratrooper Yisrael Ariel. Yisrael also witnessed the episode with the Jordanian tour guide and was that night given the duty of watching over the Dome of the Rock.

At the time Yisrael wondered to himself, "We have arrived at the threshold of the Holy Temple: we are standing at the Western Wall - where is the Messiah?"[5]

Yisrael Ariel later became a rabbi and answered his own question by becoming convinced that Israel was not called to simply wait passively for the Messiah – but should proceed to do everything they could to rebuild the Temple. His answer to the question of why the Messiah did not come in '67 was simply that Israel had not taken the steps to prepare for the Messiah's arrival.

It was this conviction that led Rabbi Yisrael to form what is today the most prominent movement to rebuild the Temple – the Temple Institute. Now 50 years later, the Temple Institute has made extensive preparations for the rebuilding of the Temple and its centre in Jerusalem is filled with vessels prepared for use in the Holy Temple.

Today, Rabbi Yisrael Ariel's Temple Institute, and Gershon Salomon's Temple Mount Faithful are both advocating for and working towards the rebuilding of the Temple. Their shared experience on the Temple Mount and their shared disappointments led to the birth of the Modern Temple Movement.

Getting Closer

While the idea of rebuilding the Temple was a fringe idea in 1967, temple activist Yehudah Glick explains that it is now becoming mainstream. "Ten years ago, there was not a single member of Knesset (the Israeli Parliament) who ascended the Temple Mount," Glick told CBN News in May 2017. "Today we have 20 Knesset members who are interested in ascending Temple Mount... and bringing the Temple Mount back into the centre of the next step in the redemption process."[6]

Although Rabbi Goren's dream of rebuilding the temple was ultimately dashed in 1967, the seeds sown in those momentous moments on the Temple Mount are today bringing Israel closer than ever to the rebuilding of her temple.

Orthodox Jews pray daily for the Third Temple to be built saying 'May it be thy will Lord God, God of our fathers, that the temple be rebuilt speedily in our days'. As we will see from the events described in the following chapters, it may well be that we are part of the generation that will see this ancient prayer fulfilled.

While the Temple Mount was handed back to Islamic control in 1967, we will see in the next chapter how Yehudah Glick - a little known temple activist - has through unlikely events risen to dramatic and unexpected prominence in Israel.

[1] For more on the 6 Day War, see Michael Oren's book *'Six Days of War: June 1967 and the Making of the Modern Middle East'*

[2] *Israel's 1967 Miracle*, CBN: Chris Mitchell, June 05, 2007

[3] Oren, Michael. *Six Days of War: June 1967 and the Making of the Modern Middle East*, Page 246

[4] *The Personal Experiences of Gershon Salomon During the 1967 Six Day War,* http://www.templemountfaithful.org/articles/gershon-salomon-and-the-1967-six-day-war.php (accessed Jan 9, 2018)

[5] *About the Temple Institute* https://www.templeinstitute.org/about.htm (accessed Jan 9, 2018)

[6] *'The Temple Mount Is in Our Hands!' Hope Reborn for the Third Temple,* CBN: Chris Mitchell, 30th May 2017, http://www1.cbn.com/cbnnews/israel/2017/may/six-day-war-victory-rekindled-hope-for-the-third-temple

4

The Stunning Rise of Yehudah Glick

October 29th, 2014 was just another day in the life of Jerusalem Rabbi and Temple Mount Activist Yehudah Glick. The soft spoken red-headed Rabbi – described by some as 'the most dangerous man in the Middle East' and by others as one who couldn't even harm a fly – had just finished giving a public lecture on "The Importance of Maintaining a Jewish Presence on the Temple Mount". Yehudah was packing his bags into the boot of his car while his wife was waiting patiently in the passenger seat. Suddenly a man on a motorcycle pulled over and asked in heavily accented Hebrew: 'Are you Yehudah Glick?". "Yes", affirmed Yehudah while his wife casually listened on from inside the car.

"I am terribly sorry," the man on the motorcycle continued with anger rising in his voice, "but you are an enemy of al-Aqsa"[1]. With that the man pulled a gun and fired four rapid shots at point blank rage into Yehudah's unprotected chest before speeding off on the motorbike.

It truly looked like the end for Rabbi Glick and the loss of one of the best spokespeople for the Temple Mount movement. While this attack was intended to spell the end for the Temple movement, we will see how it actually ended up galvanizing the movement across Israel.

Who is Yehudah Glick?

Yehudah Glick and his peers from the Temple Movement have for years been regarded as insignificant fringe elements of Israeli society with only limited influence. All this changed dramatically that day in October.

Exactly one week before the attack, doctors at the Shaarei Tzedek Medical Centre in Jerusalem worked frantically to save the life of a bullet riddled terrorist. One nurse openly questioned why they should work so hard to save the life of a man who had just killed three innocent civilians, but the rest of the team responded that they were simply doing their job.

A week later, the same team were in place as Rabbi Glick was rushed to the hospital, and the lessons learned from the week before helped them give Yehudah the best possible treatment as he was hovering between life and death. During this time many prayers were being lifted up for Rabbi Glick across Israel and the world.

In what doctors described as a miracle - none of the four bullets fired hit any vital organs. One bullet hit his spine without touching the spinal cord, while another bullet went through his neck passing within millimetres of a major artery. After only one month and having gone through nine rounds of surgery, a pale-looking Yehudah

Glick was able to leave the hospital, giving public thanks at a press conference to the 'God who raises the dead'[2].

The assassination attempt and the subsequent dramatic recovery catapulted Yehudah Glick into the national spotlight, making him a household name and breathing new impetus into the Temple Mount Movement. In fact, Yehudah's assassination attempt and subsequent recovery spawned the birth of several new organisations devoted to Jewish prayer rights on the Temple Mount.

Entering into Politics

As a member of Benjamin Netanyahu's Likud party, Rabbi Glick was listed as #56 on the ballot papers for the election of 2013. For the following election in March 2015, the newly recovered and more prominent Glick was upgraded to #33 on the ballot papers[3]. At the time, most pundits expected Netanyahu's Likud party to barely win 20 seats. Asked by the Israeli press if he would run for a more realistic place on the ballot papers, Glick explained that his wife had vetoed the decision and that he was content to stay outside of the Knesset (Israel's Parliament) and to have a merely symbolic listing on the ballot papers.

While Glick may not have planned to enter Parliament, the surprising and sweeping victory of Netanyahu in the elections brought an unexpected total of 30 Likud candidates into the Israeli Knesset.

During the course of 2016, there were several resignations from Netanyahu's party due to scandals as well as members retiring – paving the way for the very unlikely candidate Yehudah Glick to join the Knesset after all.

The rise of Yehudah Glick from the brink of death to the national spotlight, and now to the Israeli parliament is truly breathtaking to watch. It would seem that God has had a hand in the unlikely turn of events that has seen this man survive such an ordeal and now be given an increasing influence in the nation of Israel.

Slow and Steady Progress

While Yehudah Glick's entry into the Knesset may excite many Bible Prophecy observers, it does not necessarily point to a speedy rebuilding of the Temple in the near future.

Those who wish to see speedy action towards a possible rebuilding of the Temple may well find themselves disappointed in Glick's slow and steady approach.

Rabbi Glick and the Temple Institute have for years recognised the impossible political situation concerning the rebuilding of the Temple on the Temple Mount. Given the strong opposition by most orthodox Jews – and the threat of the Islamic World erupting into unparalleled levels of violence – Rabbi Glick and the Temple Institute have found it wiser to take a slow and steady approach to changing the status quo.

Yehudah Glick has since 2009 shifted away from public calls to imminently rebuild the Temple and has instead focussed his public activism on equal Jewish prayer rights on the Temple Mount. This move has helped secure broader religious support for the movement and has already helped rekindle a flame in many hearts for the Temple. This shift of focus by Yehudah and other temple activists appears to have paid off as a recent Israeli poll shows support for Jewish prayer rights on the Temple Mount hitting 50% for the first time in 2022 [4].

Asked in 2016 about the likelihood of equal prayer rights for Jews on the Temple Mount, Yehudah exclaimed "Whether it's in two years, five years or 10 years from today, I don't know. I have patience"[5].

A Sudden Green Light to Rebuild the Temple?

While Rabbi Glick and the Temple Institute both take a slow and steady approach, they none-the-less have their eye on the big picture and are awaiting the right moment to rebuild the Temple.

Rebuilding the Temple may seem impossible right now, yet the prominent role of the Temple in End Time prophecies means that we can expect a dramatic change sooner or later - which will bring about the necessary favourable environment for the rebuilding of the Temple.

Just as Yehudah Glick has had an unexpected and rapid rise to prominence, could it be that there are more unexpected developments lying ahead that will set the stage for the building of the Third Temple? Watch this space!

In the next chapter we will see how the Temple Institute is not sitting around idle waiting for this to happen. Their stated long term goal "is to do all in our limited power to bring about the building of the Holy Temple in our time". As such, they are doing everything possible to be ready including recreating and preparing vessels for the Temple and training a modern priesthood in the complex ancient Temple sacrifices and rituals.

If they are actively preparing themselves for the fulfilment of Bible prophecy, how much more should we as believers actively prepare ourselves for the Lord's return? As I have been studying these developments, I have come to a growing conviction that the Lord is coming soon – and it has led to practical changes in my life. As you read this book, may it not just be interesting information, but may it inspire you to be ready and prepared for the Lord's long promised return.

[1] *How a Palestinian Terrorist Saved the Life of Temple Mount Rabbi Yehuda Glick*, Breaking Israel News, Aug. 3, 2015 - http://www.breakingisraelnews.com/46210/how-palestinian-terrorist-saved-the-life-of-temple-mount-rabbi-yehuda-glick-inspiration/#cY62kyg6Y1x0mRBH.97

For more on Yehudah's story, see the documentary: *A Jerusalem Hug From Heaven*, https://www.youtube.com/watch?v=mrEhbinqzU (accessed Jan 18, 2018)

[2] Ibid.

[3] "Yehuda Glick is Running With The Likud - Surprised?", Arutz Sheva Israel National News, 26/2/2015 - http://www.israelnationalnews.com/News/News.aspx/191888#.VmzCQ_krLWI

[4] "Poll finds half of Jewish Israelis support Jewish prayer on Temple Mount", Jewish News Syndicate, 4/5/2022 - https://www.jns.org/poll-finds-half-of-jewish-israelis-support-jewish-prayer-on-temple-mount

[5] *Hardline US-born rabbi Yehudah Glick to enter Knesset for Likud*, Times of Israel: May 21, 2016 https://www.timesofisrael.com/hardline-us-born-rabbi-yehudah-glick-to-enter-knesset/ (accessed Jan 9 2018)

Preparing for the Temple

5

Temple Vessels and the Priesthood

Recreating the Temple Vessels

In line with their goal to do everything in their 'limited power to bring about the building of the Holy Temple', the Temple Institute has spent years faithfully and painstakingly recreating the Temple vessels. So far they have prepared more than 60 vessels[1], which can be seen on display at the Temple Institute in Jerusalem (well worth a visit!) or on their web site (www.templeinstitute.org/gallery.htm)

While visitors to the Temple Institute may get the feeling that they are visiting some sort of a museum, the pieces on display are actually fit for and intended for use in the Third Temple. Painstaking research has gone into the workmanship of each vessel to ensure it is set to the meticulous standard commanded by God in the Scriptures as well as that further documented in ancient Jewish writings such as the Talmud.

Golden Menorah

One of the most impressive vessels re-created so far is the Golden Menorah. Featuring prominently just outside the Temple Institute – it proudly faces the Temple Mount where it is hoped that it will one day stand.

The Menorah is enclosed in a special glass encasement, which is just as well as it is valued at approximately 3 million dollars! It weighs half a ton and contains 45kg of 24 karat gold.[2]

The author in front of the Golden Menorah
Author's photo

To give you an idea of the level of research involved in recreating the vessels, let me quote from what the Temple Institute writes about the process involved just to recreate the Menorah:

"After more than ten years of research and investigation, including an exhaustive study of the halachot [applications of Jewish law] concerning the design and construction of the menorah, referencing all the extant sources beginning with the Torah description itself, and including all rabbinical commentary…. up to and including contemporary texts; examining archaeological and historical evidence, including extra-rabbinic references and descriptions, (ie. Josephus Flavius); consulting metallurgical experts, goldsmiths, metal workers and electroplating experts, the Temple Institute produced a golden menorah halachically fit and ready for use in the Holy Temple...."[3]

If you multiply this level of research by the more than 60 vessels that have been recreated for the Temple so far, then you will begin to understand the enormity of the task undertaken by the Temple Institute.

Priests for the Service

While the vessels for the Temple are essential, no biblical Temple would be complete without a dedicated, trained and ritually pure priesthood.

Numbers 16:40 makes it very clear that *'no outsider, who is not a descendant of Aaron, should come near to offer incense before the Lord'*. But how, after 1900 years of exile can one find priests of Aaron's lineage to serve in the temple?

During the long exile of the Jewish people, Levites and Kohanim (descendants of Aaron) have sought to avoid intermarriage and attempted to maintain comprehensive genealogical records. The prominent Levitical Horowitz family for example have a detailed and well documented genealogy going back 1000 years, and claim a further lineage all the way back to Samuel the prophet.[4]

But how can one be sure who are the true descendants of Aaron after all these years? Modern DNA technology has proven very useful in assisting the search, and extensive studies are being done into both Levitical and Priestly lineage markers. In 1997, a breakthrough in genetic research uncovered a marker present in 98.5% of those who claim high priestly descent. Amazingly, this marker is present in individuals from both Ashkenazi (northern European) and Sephardic (Spanish / North African) Jewish family lines which have been separated geographically for close to 1000 years. The genetic trail from father to son points back to one individual who lived 3300 years ago. This individual must have been part of the priestly class, and the genetic researchers actually suggest it could well have been Aaron the High Priest himself.[5]

Against all odds, God has preserved the Jewish people during 1900 years of often traumatic exile, and they have survived horrific waves of persecution and death during the crusades, Islamic wars, religious pogroms in Russia and ultimately the holocaust. Amazingly, this DNA research appears to show that God has in addition maintained the clear unbroken lineage of a single high priestly line throughout these centuries and millennia of persecution. Could it be that against insurmountable odds, God ensured this lineage would be kept so that a true descendant of Aaron could one day serve in the re-built Temple?

Not only are priests of the correct lineage required, but they must also be trained in the extensive rituals required in the Temple. In response, the Temple Institute has started a training school for eligible Levites and Kohanim. As of December 2017, the Institute has 50 Kohanim who are thoroughly trained in the priestly service and several of whom are qualified to be High Priest.

Appointing a High Priest

In 2016, a major prophetic milestone was reached as the reconvened Israeli Sanhedrin announced that it had taken the groundbreaking step to nominate a High Priest.[6]

Believing that permission to sacrifice on the Temple Mount could come sooner than expected, the Sanhedrin knew it would be a disaster if permission was granted and no High Priest was ready to perform the crucial Day of Atonement sacrifice for the nation.

It is against this backdrop that a High Priest was nominated – for the first time since the temple was destroyed in AD 70! The nominated candidate for High Priest was Rabbi Baruch Kahane, an expert on the complicated laws pertaining to the Temple Service.

In a surprising twist, Rabbi Baruch declined the role for now, but made himself available to become the High Priest if and when the situation should arise.

A Few Hours' Notice

The Sanhedrin has called for the stockpiling of materials in a ready to assemble format for the Temple construction. It is important to note though that sacrificing on the Temple Mount does not require the prior existence of a rebuilt Temple and can be restarted before the construction has even begun. As we have seen, the Temple Institute has the vessels, the Levites, the priests and even the High Priest ready for service.

With the Temple Institute strategically located within a few minutes walking distance from the Temple Mount, Director Yisrael Ariel confidently asserts that it would only take a few hours to move the altar, the key vessels and the musical instruments across and renew the Temple service.[7]

Searching for a Holy Cow

One essential requirement is missing which could jeopardize the entire Third Temple project. It is the ashes of a 'red heifer'.

These ashes are Biblically mandated for purification in a range of situations including contact with dead bodies (Num 19). With all the bloodshed on the Temple Mount down through the centuries, the Mount itself must be cleansed before the Temple can be built.

The problem is that a pure red heifer is very rare as almost all cattle have some imperfections in their colouring. In 1996 a red heifer called 'Melody' was born. This cow was welcomed by Temple activists and generated quite an international media sensation. The Israeli left-wing media were less amused however, warning that the cow should be seen as a 'four legged bomb', potentially setting the whole region on fire. The story ended when Melody grew several white hairs at the tip of her tail and was pronounced unclean by Israeli rabbis.[8]

After several other potential finds in recent years were likewise pronounced unclean, the Temple Institute has taken matters into its own hands. In 2015 it launched a project with an experienced cattle rancher to use the powers of modern science to breed cows that meet the requirements.[9] These efforts are continuing to this present day.

It would seem that it is only a matter of time before this missing puzzle piece falls into place. Truly these developments show that the prophetic clock is ticking, and piece by piece the Temple is getting ready to be rebuilt.

In the next chapter we will look at recent infrastructure developments in and around Jerusalem. On the surface these might look like ordinary projects, but a closer look will show how these infrastructure projects are preparing the way – for the Temple, its pilgrims and ultimately for the Messiah Himself.

[1] Zeveloff, Naomi, *The Bible Is Their Textbook: Jerusalem Group Trains Priests for Third Temple,* Aug 2, 2016, Forward https://forward.com/news/israel/346591/the-bible-is-their-textbook-jerusalem-group-trains-priests-for-third-temple/ (accessed Jan 18, 2018)

[2] *The Holy Temple Menorah Today,* The Temple Institute, http://www.templeinstitute.org/history-holy-temple-menorah-1.htm (accessed Jan 5, 2018)

[3] The Temple Institute, *Building the Menorah in Our Day,* http://www.templeinstitute.org/history-holy-temple-menorah-5.htm (accessed Jan 5 2018)

[4] Wexler, Jeffrey D. *Background of R-Y2619 Ashkenazi Levites,* http://sites.google.com/site/levitedna/background-of-r1a1a-ashkenazi-levites (accessed Jan 5, 2018)

[5] Rabbi Kleiman, Yaakov. *The DNA Chain of Tradition: The Discovery of the "Cohen Gene"* www.cohen-levi.org/jewish_genes_and_genealogy/the_dna_chain_of_tradition.htm (accessed Jan 5, 2018)

[6] Berkowitz, Adam Eliyahu. *Sanhedrin Appoints High Priest in Preparation for Third Temple,* Breaking Israel News, Aug 29, 2016 https://www.breakingisraelnews.com/74772/sanhedrin-appoints-high-priest-preparation-third-temple/ (accessed Jan 2, 2018)

[7] *Could Hanukkah Happen Today?* Dec 18, 2017 https://www.breakingisraelnews.com/99488/hanukkah-happen-today

[8] Rosenberg, Joel. *Epicenter: Why the current rumblings in the Middle East Will Change Your Future,* Page 196

[9] *"Red Heifers In Israel Prompt 3rd Temple Speculation",* Jul 18, 2015: http://www.wnd.com/2015/07/red-heifers-in-israel-prompt-3rd-temple-speculation/

(accessed Jan 2, 2018)

6

Preparing the Way (literally)

In the days of the first and second Temple, Jews from all over Israel – and later also from surrounding countries – would make a pilgrimage up to the Temple three times a year as commanded in the Scripture.

This pilgrimage ritual saw massive crowds converge on Jerusalem. Based on the number of Passover lambs that were sacrificed, Josephus estimated the arrival of 3 million pilgrims during Passover at his time!

Today, Israel's minister of Transportation, Yisroel Katz, is in charge of an infrastructure upgrade to build an express train route to ferry travelers from Tel Aviv and Ben Gurion airport to Jerusalem.

Hannah Katan, a recent convert to the Temple movement describes her sense of excitement at these plans. She explains with a big smile "It's here, we feel it. All the trains that are being built from Tel Aviv to Jerusalem, the highway that is being widened to six lanes, the light rail in Jerusalem – what's all this for?" Answering her own question, she continues "So that we can all ascend, as one, to the Temple".[1]

Indeed, Transportation Minister Yisroel Katz has stated that facilitating a massive transportation of Jews to the Temple Mount for the Jewish feasts is part of his vision for the project. According to Breaking Israel News, the minister explained his motivation by saying 'As a Kohen (Jew of the priestly caste) I have a special connection to the holy site. In front of my eyes I constantly see the words 'Prepare the way, prepare the way...'" Indeed the final stop for the train line will be the "Kotel/Har Habayit Stop" (Western Wall/Temple Mount Stop).[2]

In a similar vein, Jerusalem Mayor Nir Barkat has announced plans to build a cable car system. The cable cars will depart from Emek Refaim Train station to the Western Wall and the Temple Mount and will be capable of transporting thousands of people per hour. The Israeli government ministers approved this plan during a cabinet meeting held inside the Western Wall Tunnels.

While these plans all fit with the overall goal of modernizing Jerusalem, they could also fit the purpose of creating the infrastructure necessary for the resumption of the Biblical pilgrimage to the Temple.

Preparing the Way for the Messiah

Ultimately, all the work involved in recreating the temple vessels, training the priests and building transport infrastructure to Jerusalem is all about one thing – preparing for the Messianic age.

While Orthodox Jews and Christians disagree on the identity of the Messiah – and whether it will be His first or second visit to earth (!) – both groups see the link between the re-built Temple and the Messianic age to come.

According to Bible teacher Jan Markel, the level of Messianic expectancy in the Jewish community is actually higher than in the Christian community[3]. This was exemplified when an Israeli radio station in 2016 broadcast a breathtaking report of the Messiah's arrival in Jerusalem, complete with cheering crowds in the background. The recording was staged and the radio channel made an effort to make sure listeners knew, yet it sounded so convincing that many called the station to check if it was real![4]

Echoing this level of expectancy, the Israeli commissioner of police, Ron Alsheikh, revealed that his department were considering the extra security measures needing to be in place for the arrival of the Messiah.[5]

While we as Christians don't believe the Messiah will need security arrangements – He will provide His own security(!) – it is none-the-less interesting to observe the level of interest displayed by the Jewish community regarding this.

As the Temple mount developments keep gathering pace, may the Jewish people who are looking for the Messiah, come to a realization that He has already come once – and is indeed coming again soon! Also, may the Christian community awaken from self-centered slumber, and make herself ready as a bride for her coming Bridegroom....

Having spent the last few chapters looking at the detailed preparations taking place in Jerusalem, we will in the next chapters look at the role of the Third Temple in Bible Prophecy.

Buckle up as it's going to be quite a ride!

[1] Sharon, Itamar. *The women waiting, and weaving, for the Third Temple*, Aug 15, 2016: https://www.timesofisrael.com/the-women-waiting-and-weaving-for-the-third-temple/ (accessed Jan 18, 2018)

[2] Wander, Joshua, *Infrastructure to Bring Millions of Pilgrims to Temple Mount Quietly Being Constructed*, Breaking Israel News June 27, 2017
https://www.breakingisraelnews.com/90393/infrastructure-bring-millions-pilgrims-temple-mount-quietly-constructed (accessed Dec 31, 2017)

[3] *Police in Israel actively preparing for Messiah's arrival*, Aug 1, 2017
http://www.wnd.com/2017/01/israeli-police-preparing-for-messiah/ (accessed Jan 18, 2018)

[4] Berkowitz, Adam Eliyahu. *Radio Station Announces Arrival of Messiah in Jerusalem*, Aug 17, 2016
https://www.breakingisraelnews.com/74094/breaking-news-flash-messiah-arrived-not-really/ (accessed Jan 18, 2018)

[5] *Police in Israel actively preparing for Messiah's arrival*, Op Cit

The Temple in Prophecy

7

Daniel's 70 Weeks

In exile, the prophet Daniel studied the writings of Jeremiah the prophet. He must have been intrigued when he came across Jeremiah's prophecy of a 70 year exile (Jer 29:10) and amazed when he did the calculations and worked out that the 70 years of exile were almost over.

Being a man of prayer and great humility, Daniel then began to pray and fast for Israel's restoration, confessing his sins and those of his people.

It was in this context that God revealed to Daniel a prophetic outline of the events leading up to the Messiah's first and second comings. The outline was based on 'seventy weeks', or more literally 'seventy sevens' of years.

According to Daniels prophecy, there would be 69 'weeks' from the 'command to restore and rebuild Jerusalem' until 'Messiah the prince' (Dan 9:25). Based on the 360 day calendars used by both the Jews and the Babylonians at the time, Chuck Missler calculates that there would have been 69x7x360 = 173'880 days from this declaration until the Messiah was supposed to come.

Missler further points to the declaration to rebuild Jerusalem by Artaxerxes on March 14, 445BC. By adding 173'880 days to this date, he arrives at April 6, 32 AD as the day for the Messiah's arrival. Missler further shows that this could have been the very day when Jesus triumphantly rode into Jerusalem as her Messiah before His subsequent rejection[1].

Not only did Daniel's revelation relate to the first coming of the Messiah, but it also revealed details about His second coming. Most Bible prophecy scholars agree that the 70th 'week' still needs to be fulfilled. According to Daniel 9:27, during this final 7 year period:

- A 7 year covenant will be made with the antichrist
- The covenant will be broken after 3½ years
- The Temple sacrifices will be stopped

The 7 year period will end with a final judgment of the anti-christ (see also Dan 11:45).

We should note carefully these verses do not state that the antichrist will build the Temple. Nor does it explicitly say that the 7 year treaty will cause the Temple to be built. Many Bible teachers speculate that this could happen, but let's remember that this is simply an assumption, and that the actual events might unfold quite differently.

In summary, Daniel's 70 week prophecy gave a timeline for the coming of the Messiah and for the final 7 years of this age. While

Daniel's prophecy does not state who will build the Temple, it assumes that the Temple of God will be in opeation performing ritual sacrifices prior to the second half of the final 7 year period of this age.

Daniel 11:31 further states that after the sacrifices are stopped, *'the abomination of desolation'* will be erected. What does this puzzling phrase mean? In the next chapter, I will endeavor to give some insight into this phrase by looking at dramatic events from 175BC. We will also see how the events of those days serve as solemn warnings to both Christians and Jews as we move into the End Times.

[1] Missler, Chuck. *The Precision of Prophecy: Daniels 70 Weeks* http://www.khouse.org/articles/2004/552/ (accessed Jan 19, 2018)

8

Hanukkah and the Abomination of Desolation

"And forces shall be mustered by him, and they shall defile the sanctuary fortress; then they shall take away the daily sacrifices, and place there the abomination of desolation." Daniel 11:31

What is the Abomination of Desolation?

The exact nature of this puzzling phrase has long been debated by Bible scholars. Some scholars argue that the 'abomination of desolation' took place at the Roman siege of Jerusalem in AD 70. During the siege, the Roman general Titus set up an idolatrous Roman ensign on the Temple Mount. According to Daniel Morais, this stood there for 3½ years before the Temple was destroyed, putting an end to sacrifices and offerings[1].

Some 40 years earlier, Jesus had warned His followers to flee Jerusalem *"when you see the 'abomination of desolation' spoken of by Daniel the prophet, standing in the holy place"* (Matt 24:15-16). One problem with the view that this Roman ensign was the Abomination of Desolation, is that by the time it was erected all escape routes had been cut off and the city was doomed.

Another problem with this view is that the ensign was not erected in the Holy place of the Temple as foretold by Jesus. Furthermore, this desecration of the Temple did not happen in the context of any 7-year peace treaty with Israel as foretold by Daniel (Dan 9:27, 11:31). We can therefore see that the Roman siege of Jerusalem in AD 70 does not correlate well with the description of the Abomination of Desolation.

Many Bible scholars believe therefore that this abomination will be a future event, while disagreeing over exactly what this event will be. Carl Gallups for example suggests that the 'abomination of desolation' could mark an end time defilement of the Church[2]. However, it is clear that both Daniel's and Jesus' original Jewish listeners would not have understood His statement this way and would have expected a literal defilement of a literal Temple.

Carl Gallups also suggests that the present day Islamic Dome of the Rock could be the abomination of desolation. But this ignores the statement of Jesus that when you '*see the "abomination of desolation,".... then let those who are in Judea flee to the mountains*' (Matt 24:15-16). If the Dome of the Rock is the abomination of desolation, then Jesus' followers should have been living hiding in the mountains since the 7th century AD when it was constructed!

To clear up the confusion around this puzzling phrase, we are going to delve back into a dark chapter of Israel's history which remains unknown to many Christians. The incident which we will describe frames the context of Jesus' reference to the 'Abomination of Desolation', and gives us essential insight into this pivotal End Times event.

A Prophetic Precursor

In AD 175BC, 400 years after Daniel wrote down his prophecies, Antiochus IV Ephiphanes became ruler over the dominant and powerful Greco-Syrian empire to the north of Israel. His reign ushered in a time which has been described by many scholars as the clearest prophetic foreshadowing of the antichrist in Israel's history.

At the time of Antiochus, Greek Hellenism was a powerful force on the global stage. Even many Israelites were seduced by the magnetic, materialistic, pleasure seeking and idol worshipping culture of the Greeks.

Jason - a Hellenised and corrupt Levitical priest - entered into a treaty with Antiochus, which enabled Jason to become High Priest in Jerusalem. In exchange Jason helped erect an idol in Jerusalem and built a gymnasium in town – a place that openly promoted homosexual activity. Jason's actions divided Israel - outraging those who remained faithful to the Torah, while many Hellenised Jews rallied to Jason's side.

Meanwhile, Antiochus was pre-occupied with his intense rivalry with the southern Ptolemaic kingdom in Egypt. This rivalry was predicted in great detail in Daniel 11's prophesied wars between the 'king of the north and the king of the south'.

Three years after the treaty with Jason the High Priest, Antiochus - who called himself 'Epiphanes' or the "god man made flesh"

- suffered a humiliating loss in battle against his arch-rivals in Egypt (predicted in Dan 11:30).

Returning from this stinging defeat, he heard of insurrection and trouble brewing in Israel. Entering the city of Jerusalem under the guise of peace, the infuriated Antiochus launched a vicious surprise attack on its inhabitants. The book of Maccabees records that when the dust had settled 80'000 Jews had been butchered. Not satisfied, Antiochus proceeded to defile the Holy of Holies in the Temple – sacrificing a pig on the altar of God and pouring swine broth over the holy vessels and holy parchments.

The Abomination of Desolation

Antiochus decreed an end to the daily sacrifices in the temple and erected an idol of Zeus in the Holy place. Going one step further, Antiochus replaced the face of Zeus on the idol with an image of himself.

This hideous idol was called by the Jews in those days the 'abomination of desolation' – based on the prophecy of Daniel 11:31.

The idol was not just an abomination, but it also become the source of great desolation. As soon as the idol was erected, intense house-to-house persecution broke out across the entire land of Israel. Houses were searched meticulously, and those found keeping God's laws were mercilessly tortured and killed.

Daniel 11:33 predicted that many of the faithful would fall by the sword. The apocryphal books Maccabees I and II give us a graphic description of what happened in those days. One example is the story of the elderly scribe Eleazer. Eleazer's captors desired to treat him kindly due to his advanced age and implored him to only pretend to go along with their demands. Eleazer however refused to compromise and went willingly to a torturous death, setting an example that was to be followed by many - young and old, men, women and children in the days to come. These precious Jewish heroes who paid such a high price for their faith could well be those that the writer of Hebrews refers to when he talks of those who *'were tortured, not accepting deliverance, that they might obtain a better resurrection'* (Heb 11:35).

Antiochus' plan to hellenize Israel seemed to be slowly but surely working. Much was truly at stake, for if Antiochus' diabolical plan had succeeded, then there would have been no distinct nation of Israel, no books of the Law, no Temple and no one keeping or knowing God's commandments by the time Jesus was to be born 150 years later. But in these dark days of suffering, a small group of rebels began the counterattack.

400 years earlier, Daniel had predicted, *'the people who know their God shall be strong, and carry out great exploits'* (Dan 11:32). Truly this is what happened as the rebels under the command of Judah Maccabee gradually gained strength. Although they were hopelessly outnumbered and facing undoubtedly the greatest super-power of their day, Judah and his men were undaunted through firm faith in God. Antiochus sent wave after wave of soldiers to crush the rebellion – yet time and again Judah emerged victorious. Finally, Antiochus sent 47'000 men to squash Judah's rag-tag army of around 3'000 men once and for all.

Hearing of the impending onslaught, Judah and his men first spent a day in fasting and repentance, where Judah reminded his men of the great victories of Israel in the Bible. The next day the Maccabees launched a surprise attack on the main enemy camp. Against all odds they delivered yet another crushing blow to their enemies. After 3 years of battles and stunning military wins, the brave Maccabees finally retook Jerusalem, cleansed the Temple and re-dedicated it to the God of Israel. On his way back to Israel to fight the Maccabees once again, Antiochus was struck down by an intestinal disease and died an agonizing and humiliating death[3].

The miraculous victory of the Maccabees has been commemorated ever since as the feast of Hanukkah. At Hanukkah the Jewish people say to each other that 'a great miracle happened here'. Truly this was a great miracle, and one which ultimately prepared the way of the Messiah's birth in Bethlehem some 150 years later.

If there had been no Hanukkah – if there had been no Jewish heroes willing to lay down their lives for their belief in God and to fight for their beliefs – there would have been no Christmas, no Bible and ultimately no one to receive and propagate the message of Israel's Messiah.

Hanukkah as a Prophetic Precursor

While the story of Hanukkah is fascinating, what does it have to do with the End Time rebuilding of the Temple?

The answer is found in Jesus' statement in Matt 24:15 that in the End Times we will again *'see the Abomination of Desolation in the Holy Place'*. Bible believers in the days of Jesus could have been excused for thinking that the prophecies of Daniel 11 and the abomination of desolation were a closed chapter fulfilled during the dark days of Antiochus.

Many would therefore have been surprised by Jesus' statement. Jesus went on further to state that the return of the abomination of desolation would mark a renewed time of intense persecution when they should again flee to the mountains (Matt 24:16-22).

Many leading Bible scholars therefore see Hanukkah as being the clearest prophetic foreshadowing in Israel's history of the End Times and the coming antichrist. By studying Hanukkah, we can therefore gain valuable insights into the End Times conflict which will once again be centered on the Temple.

Hanukkah and the End Times

The reign of Antiochus bears many parallels to the End Times and carries powerful lessons for the final end time generation.

Just like the time of Hanukkah, Paul tells us that the End Times will be characterized by a *'great falling away'* (2 Thes 2:3). The very same sensual Greek spirit that was behind the falling away at the time of Hanukkah is increasingly pervasive in our modern Western societies. The Greeks promoted body image, materialism, pleasure and homosexuality. A brief glance at our modern culture reveals the very same spirit active in almost all entertainment and media. While the Greeks built gymnasiums, our western societies have in recent years seen gyms and fitness clubs popping up on seemingly every street corner and in most shopping centers. While it is good to keep fit, is the growth of gyms a symptom of the increasing focus on body image and sensuality in our culture?

Those who embraced Greek values in the days of Hanukkah were seen as modern and enlightened, and those who held Biblical values were seen as old-fashioned stumbling blocks to progress. The days of Antiochus came to be marked by vicious persecution of the true saints, and many End Time prophecies predict a similar time of persecution in the final days before the Lord's return. The parallels with our modern society are striking as 'progressives' across the Western world rage against conservative values and those who hold firm to biblical worldviews. It doesn't seem too farfetched to imagine that persecution could arise from those who embrace seemingly tolerant progressive values.

I personally believe that persecution is coming, and that the church in the West has to get ready to face difficult times. Just as the church has to be ready for the Lord's return, so we also have to be ready to face persecution as we stand for the truth of God's Word. As Paul the Apostle said, *'all who desire to live godly in Christ Jesus will suffer persecution'* (2 Tim. 3:12). It is becoming increasingly unpopular to stand for Biblical values but may we - like the heroes of Hanukkah - count the cost and remain faithful to our Lord no matter what lies ahead.

When we read of the heroism of the martyrs of Hanukkah, we can feel that we would never be able to follow in their footsteps. But I believe that the God who gave them strength in those difficult days, will in the same way give us supernatural strength to face whatever difficulties lie ahead. So, let's look to God and allow Him to be our source of strength in difficult times. Let us hold on to the promise of Daniel for these difficult times – that *those who know their God shall be strong and carry out great exploits'* (Dan 11:32).

Hanukkah's Warning to the Jewish people

In the days of Hanukkah, the nation of Israel was divided between those who wanted Israel to be like the nations of the world, and those who held firm to Torah values. Those who had compromised their values were those who pushed for and entered into the 'peace treaty' with Antiochus which ultimately became so disastrous for the nation.

The same conflict over values is increasingly manifesting in Israel today with the ever-widening gap between radical left-wing atheist Israelis and the numerically strong and religiously conservative orthodox block.

In the midst of this struggle for national identity and purpose, Israel faces ongoing and relentless pressure to reach a peace deal with the Palestinians. Foreign diplomats from practically every nation on the planet are continually pressuring Israel to enter into a peace treaty on terms that would drastically weaken Israel's very own security. The left wing of Israeli politics is in great danger of entering into such a treaty in their desire for Israel to finally find acceptance among the nations of the world.

As Israel celebrates the Feast of Hanukkah every year, she is repeatedly reminded of the danger of compromising and entering into a treaty with a foreign ruler in order to secure peace.

Hanukkah and the End Times

Hanukkah's similarities with the End Times are many. Just like Antiochus had a treaty with Israel, so will the antichrist. Just like Antiochus suddenly broke the treaty and unleashed devastation on Israel, the antichrist will do likewise. Just like Antiochus tried to replace Temple Worship with the worship of his image, so Paul tells us that the *'son of perdition'* will in the End Times *'sit in the temple of God showing himself that he is God'* (2 Thes 2:3-4).

Going further, Antiochus' erection of the Abomination of Desolation in the Temple marked a period of intense persecution – and the antichrist's end time defilement of the Temple will do the same. Antiochus was struck down not by man, but by God. And in this way, the antichrist too will meet his final end.

After all its desecration and filth, the Temple was rededicated to God. And so, after the defeat of the antichrist, the Temple will be restored. The defeat of Antiochus paved the way for the birth of Jesus and Him coming to the Temple. Likewise the defeat of the antichrist will lead to Jesus' return to His House in Jerusalem.

The Pattern Continues

In this chapter we have seen how Hanukkah is a dramatic prophetic pattern for the End Times struggle over the Temple Mount. We have specifically seen how the 'Abomination of Desolation' is best understood to refer to a literal idol which will stand in a literal future Temple. This is one of the clearest Biblical evidences that there will indeed be a Third Temple standing in the End Times.

In the next chapter we will see how Hanukkah also sets a framework helping us identify the kind of leader which will ultimately enable Israel to rebuild the temple.

[1] Morais, Daniel, *The Abomination that Causes Desolation Explained,* http://revelationrevolution.org/the-abomination-that-causes-desolation-explained/ (accessed Jan 22, 2018)

[2] *Red heifers in Israel prompt 3rd Temple speculation*, World Net Daily, July 18, 2015: http://www.wnd.com/2015/07/red-heifers-in-israel-prompt-3rd-temple-speculation/ (accessed Jan 9, 2018)

[3] For more on the Hanukkah story, see the books of Maccabees I and II that are part of the Apocrypha.

9

The Architect – Cyrus or the AntiChrist?

As we have seen in the previous chapter, the New Testament foretells a defilement of the rebuilt Temple by the 'son of perdition... (sitting) as God in the temple of God' (2 Thes 2:4).

How will the Temple be re-built?

The building of the Third Temple seems impossible in the present political climate. Many End Time teachers have therefore suggested that the Temple could be built as part of a 7-year peace treaty with the antichrist.

This possible association with the antichrist, obviously leaves a bad taste in any believers' mouth! Why should we as Christians support the rebuilding of the Temple based on a false peace with the antichrist himself! Some would therefore say that the End Time temple is an antichrist temple and any involvement with it is almost tantamount to a denial of Christ.

These are serious charges but are all based on the assumption that the Temple will be rebuilt from a peace treaty with the antichrist. We should take note that nowhere in the Bible does it explicitly say that it will happen this way.

While some have asserted that the Third Temple will be 'an antichrist temple', the late Grant Jeffrey pointed out how the Bible itself consistently refers to it as the 'Temple of God' (Rev 11:1, 2 Thes 2:4) and Jesus Himself spoke of the 'holy place' in this Temple (Matt 24:15)[1].

Joel Richardson likewise points out that the Temple cannot be desecrated unless it truly sacred to God in the first place.[2]

It will therefore appear that the antichrist will not be the one who initiates the building of the Third Temple.

If so, then who else could it be?

The Cyrus Factor

Let's return to the End Times prophetic pattern set by the events of Hanukkah. The events of Hanukkah were framed by the return of the Jews from exile in Babylon some 300 years earlier. This return and the rebuilding of the Temple was thanks to the decree by the divinely appointed gentile King Cyrus. While King Cyrus is mostly known for helping bring the Jews back from exile, he described his divine mandate as being to *'build Him [God] a house at Jerusalem'* (Ezra 1:2)

So the pattern of Hanukkah is that the Temple was built not long after the Jewish return from exile, and the crucial go-ahead to build the Temple was granted by the leader of the super-power of the day,

King Cyrus of Persia. Furthermore, the Temple was built some time before its ultimate desolation by Antiochus.

We have seen that the Temple won't be an 'antichrist Temple', but rather a genuine, sacred Temple of God. Could it therefore be that following the Hanukkah pattern, God will raise up another friendly ruler like Cyrus of old? A leader of a super-power who through his power and influence would open the doors towards the rebuilding of the Temple?

President Trump and Jerusalem

A number of US based Christian leaders, routinely compared America's 45th President to the Biblical King Cyrus foretold in Isaiah 45 [3]. They pointed out that although King Cyrus did not know the God of Israel, God appointed him by name with the mandate to fulfil God's divine purposes. A primary part of Cyrus' divine calling was to order the rebuilding of the Temple in Jerusalem (Isaiah 44:28, Ezra 1:2).

Trump's bold Jerusalem embassy declaration was one of the most unexpected moves of his presidency. It was hailed by Israel's Temple activists, who saw this announcement as a big step towards recognizing and supporting the rebuilding of the Temple[4]. Trump's declaration has also sparked debate in Israel and has strengthened the Israeli desire to reclaim her entire biblical heritage including the Temple Mount.

Furthermore, Trump initiated the 'Abraham Accords' a movement that has propelled Israel into a historic flourishing friendship with several of its Arab neighbours including Bahrain and the UAE.

It has even marked the warming of relations with Saudi Arabia, with the powerful Saudi Crown Prince Mohammad bin Salman declaring Israel as a potential ally[5].

Could it be that Trump's bold stand regarding Jerusalem and his 'Abraham Accords' initiative has set in motion changes on the ground that will lead to the rebuilding of the Temple?

Jewish leaders have pointed out that the gematria (numerical value) of Donald Trump's name equals that of the phrase 'Meshiach Ben David' (Messiah, Son of David). These same rabbis are quick to point out that they do not believe that Trump is the Messiah (just as well!). They view the gematria of Trump's name as an indication of him playing a role in the 'redemptive process' – a role in preparing the conditions for the arrival of the Messiah. What could better prepare the way for the Messiah than the rebuilding of the Temple?

Summary

We have seen that the antichrist is unlikely to be the facilitator of the Third Temple. Following the pattern of Hanukkah, God may be raising up a bold, strong and friendly international leader who will enable Israel to fulfil her prophetic and biblical mandate.

It is too early to tell exactly how it will all come together, but we as Christians are called to do more than simply watch these developments. Let us take our place in prayer that God's purposes and promises will be fulfilled here on earth – and specifically in Jerusalem – preparing the way for the Lord's coming.

Having considered the 'Cyrus factor', let's look at how the Islamic world will react to the building of the Third Temple. In the next chapter we will look at this question in the context of gaining an understanding of the role of Islam in the End Times.

[1] Grant, Jeffrey. *The New Temple and the Second Coming*, Page 90

[2] *Red heifers in Israel prompt 3rd Temple speculation,* Jul 18, 2015 http://www.wnd.com/2015/07/red-heifers-in-israel-prompt-3rd-temple-speculation/ (accessed Jan 19, 2018)

[3] Lance Wallnau. *Why Trump Is 'God's Chaos Candidate' and 'Wrecking Ball',* CBN News: Mar 21, 2017, https://www1.cbn.com/cbnnews/us/2017/march/lance-wallnau-weighs-in-on-gods-chaos-candidate-now-americas-president (accessed Jan 14, 2018)

[4] Berkowitz, Adam Eliyahu. *Trump's Jerusalem Declaration 'Enormous Step Towards Bringing Third Temple',* Dec. 7, 2017
https://www.breakingisraelnews.com/99002/trumps-jerusalem-declaration-next-step-third-temple (accessed Jan 19, 2018)

[5] *Saudi Crown prince says Israel 'potential ally',* France 24, Mar 3, 2022 https://www.france24.com/en/live-news/20220303-saudi-crown-prince-says-israel-potential-ally (accessed May 12, 2022)

10

Islam and the Temple

If a friendly foreign leader – like a Cyrus figure – backed Israel in building the temple, how then would the Islamic world react?

In this chapter we will first deal briefly with the possible role of Islam in End Time prophecy. With this in mind, we will then examine how the Islamic world might respond to the rise of the Third Temple.

Islam and End Times

Islam Expert and End Times teacher Joel Richardson has uncovered a significant correlation between Islamic and Christian understandings of the End Times.

The Islamic world is expecting its own 'Messiah' known as the Mahdi to appear in the End Times. According to Joel, this expected Mahdi has stunning similarities to what the Biblical antichrist will be doing. He will wage war against Jews and Christians, will conquer Jerusalem and will reign the world for a 7-year period. Amazingly Islamic teachers expect the Mahdi to have a returned Jesus by his side who will persuade all to submit to Islam and follow the Mahdi.[1] Any such 'Jesus' would obviously be a false prophet by the biblical standard. Christian eschatology speaks precisely of such a figure accompanying the antichrist and performing great signs and wonders to deceive many.

At the very least, it would seem that these End Times teachings of Islam are setting up the Muslim world to accept the coming of the antichrist and to side with him against Israel and true Christians.

However intriguing we may find these Islamic teachings, our foundation for understanding the End Times has to be squarely based on the Bible. Does the Bible itself predict a role for Islam in the End Times?

While the traditional view of End Times prophecy is that the final antichrist empire will arise out of Europe, Joel Richardson builds a fascinating case for it coming out of the Islam dominated Middle Eastern nations.

In brief he points out that:

- We should view the Bible through a Middle Eastern lens rather than a European/Western lens
- The events of the Bible all took place in the Middle East
- End times prophecies likewise involve the Middle East. Messiah's return is consistently linked with Him rescuing Israel from her enemies and pouring judgement on the nations that come against her. These nations are specified by name, and include Middle Eastern nations such as Edom and Moab which make up modern day Jordan (Num 24:14-20, Is. 25:8-11),

Syria and her capital Damascus (Is 17), Egypt (Is 19), Turkey (Ezek 30:1-5) and the Philistine areas (Ezek 25:12-17).
- While the revived Roman Empire theory is based on a generally accepted view of Daniel's prophecies, through a careful historical and textual study Joel builds a case that a revived Middle-Eastern Islamic Empire may be a closer fit to Daniel's utterances.[2]

While we may not agree with all of Joel's findings, serious students of Bible prophecy would do well to examine Joel's views and keep them in mind as we approach the End Times.

Islam and the Temple

The Islamic world strongly opposes a Jewish presence in Jerusalem and especially any Jewish activity on the Temple Mount. But how then can the Third Temple be built?

Some prophecy teachers have envisioned Islam collapsing in an upcoming war, thus paving the way for the rebuilding of the Temple. This could be the case and would certainly fit the traditional view of the antichrist empire emerging out of Europe to dominate the world.

However, if Joel's view is correct then the Islamic world will instead continue to grow in strength and influence until it one day becomes the seat of the antichrist's empire. Such a global rise of Islam would obviously have profound implications for the world in terms of rising persecution of both Christians and Jews. For the purpose of our study, it raises the question of how the Third Temple could possibly be built under the imposing shadow of Islam?

A Compromise with Islam?

Interestingly, several Temple Mount groups see co-operation with Islam as a real possibility and believe it to a harbinger of a new age of global peace.[3]

Yehudah Glick, the increasingly prominent face of the Temple Mount Movement, has been actively involved in such interfaith dialogue and believes that the temple should be a 'house of prayer for all nations'.

Many of us might have thought that the assassination attempt on Yehudah's life would have put an end to his interfaith ideas. Shockingly, barely ten months after the attempt on his life, Glick was invited to Turkey. There he was celebrated as the guest of honour at a Ramadan celebration attended by 1000 Muslim Clerics.[4]

His host and the organizer of the event was the high profile Turkish Muslim writer and TV personality Adnan Oktar. Adnan has for several years been publicly calling for Jews, Christians and Muslims to support the rebuilding of the Jewish temple[5]. Drawing on Islamic prophecies, Adnan proclaims that the Jewish Temple should be rebuilt and that Muslims are obliged to support the project.

Glick appears wide open to the idea of working together with Islamic leaders for the building of the Third Temple. Glick has spoken of the possibility of the Dome of the Rock becoming the Holy of Holies in the rebuilt Temple – a house of prayer for all who believe in one God![6]

Many Bible-believing Christians and sections of the Temple movement strongly disagree that the Temple worship could in any way be shared with the Islamic faith. It is interesting to note in this context that Revelation 11:1-2 describe the outer court of the Third Temple as being '*given to the gentiles*', perhaps indicating some kind of shared arrangement on the Temple Mount as envisaged by Glick and certain Muslim leaders.

Summary

Large portions of the Islamic world are dead set against any temple being built on the Temple Mount. It is none the less possible that the Third Temple could come after some kind of compromise with influential Islamic leaders.

This kind of compromise is unpalatable to many believers. However, we need to keep in mind that no matter what kind of compromise might be happening behind the scenes, the Third Temple will be sacred to God and will be called 'the Temple of God' (2 Thes 2:4).

It is too early to say exactly how Islam will fit into this picture and into the End Time puzzle. Let's remember though that Muslims are not our enemy, and that most of them were born into Islam with no choice or freedom to leave the religion. Let us continue to pray for revival in the Islamic world and for many of them to have dreams, visions and revelations of Jesus.

In the next chapter we will look at whether Christian should be involved in supporting the building of the Third Temple in Jerusalem.

[1] Richardson, Joel. *The Islamic Anti-Christ,* Los Angeles, CA: WND Books, 2009

[2] For more see Richardson, Joel. *MidEast Beast, The Scriptural Case for an Islamic Anti-Christ,* Washington DC: WND Books, 2012

[3] See a striking example of this approach at www.godsholymountain.org

[4] "Temple Mount Activist 'Survives' Dinner - With 1,000 Muslims", Arutz Sheva Israel National News, Jun 7, 2015 http://www.israelnationalnews.com/News/News.aspx/197769#.Vm0zsfnRKko (accessed Jan 19, 2018)

[5] Richardson, Joel. *End Time Eyewitness*, WND: 2014. Available from wnfilms.com

[6] Ibid.

Christians and the Temple

11

Can Christians Support the Rebuilding of the Temple?

In October 2007, on the last day of the Feast of Tabernacles, a group of 34 West Papuans showed up at the Temple Institute in Jerusalem. Influenced by Christian pro-Israel missionaries, the group had come to donate towards the Third Temple project.

As Temple Institute CEO Rabbi Yisrael Ariel saw the nature of the donation he became emotional – it was one kilogram of solid gold, plus a large sum of money! Some of the members of the delegation even began taking off their jewelry to donate – one couple even giving their wedding rings to the Temple Institute. West Papua is rich in gold, and the delegation declared that although this was their first donation, there would be more to follow.[1]

The West Papuan delegation explained their donation as being motivated by a verse in the prophet Zechariah: *"Even those from afar shall come and build the Temple of the Lord."* (Zec 6:15)

But how can Christians be involved in rebuilding the Temple, if we truly believe that we no longer need sacrifices or temple rituals to be right with God – as Jesus is the ultimate sacrifice?

To better understand the answer to this question, we will look briefly at the role played by Christians in Israel's modern-day restoration. We will also look at the nature and meaning of the sacrificial system.

The Christian Role in Israel's Restoration

Christians have played a significant role in the modern restoration of Israel.

In 1898 it was the influential Rev. William Hechler who opened political doors and gave international legitimacy to the fledgling Zionist movement.

In 1917, it was the work of Christian Zionists in the British parliament that brought about the significant Balfour Declaration – paving the way for the re-birth of the modern state of Israel.

During the Holocaust, it was often Christians who - because of their beliefs - risked their lives to hide and protect persecuted Jews.

In more modern times, Christians have played a key role in bringing home Jewish people to the nation of Israel. For example, the Christian organization Ebenezer Operation Exodus has brought home over 160'000 Jews to Israel since its inception in 1991.

Jesus will truly not return again until His people are back in His land – and are welcoming Him back with the messianic phrase

'Blessed is He who comes in the Name of the Lord' (Matt 23:31). So, Christian supporters of Israel will argue that helping Israel in these various practical areas is ultimately part of preparing the way for the Lord's return. Is aiding the Temple Mount movement any different?

Did Jesus do away with the Sacrificial System?

The typical Christian understanding of the sacrificial system is that animals had to die for the sins of the people in order that mankind could approach the holiness of God. The death of Jesus was the final and ultimate sacrifice taking away our sins. Therefore, any further sacrifices can be seen as 'blasphemous' towards the work Jesus has accomplished. Add to this the view that the coming Temple will be an antichrist Temple, and you have a theological framework which has caused many believers to shun any involvement in the Third Temple project.

We have in chapter 9 explained why this Third Temple will not be an antichrist Temple and will in fact be genuinely holy to God. In order to address the other part of the question related to the sacrificial system, we will briefly examine the meaning and purpose of the sacrifices.

The first important fact to be aware of is that not all sacrifices were for sin. In fact, only two out of the five specified sacrifices were specifically for sin (Lev. chapters 1-5).

The meaning of the Hebrew word for sacrifice brings further clarity on the purpose of the sacrificial system. The English word 'sacrifice' implies something (possibly costly) given to a god, and often carries the idea of appeasing an angry deity. However, the

Hebrew word for sacrifice 'korban' comes from a word meaning to 'draw near'.

According to author and Messianic teacher Daniel Lancaster, the 'sin offering' is best understood as a 'purification offering' as it was also required in situations where no 'sin' was committed – such as childbirth or the completion of a Nazarite vow[2]. Furthermore, the sin offering and the trespass offering both required confession of sin and restitution or repayment of what was taken (in other words, repentance). It was only once these acts of repentance were done that sin was forgiven and atonement was made (Lev. 5:16).

If the animal sacrifices in and of themselves could have taken away sin, then Jesus' death merely gives us a convenient way to avoid performing any more animal sacrifices. But Jesus' death was not to save more animals from dying – it was on a totally different level as the once and only offering to cleanse us from sin and make a new and living way for us to draw close to God.

We have seen that the sin offerings themselves could not take away sin and that the sin offering is better seen as a way of drawing near to God through ritual purification after repentance has taken place. Therefore, the Apostle Paul had no problem performing the sacrifices of the Nazarite vow even after the death of Jesus, even though this sacrifice includes a sin offering (Acts 21:26). This also help explain how according to Ezekiel's prophecies, there will be a Temple standing in the Millennium performing animal sacrifices during the reign of Messiah on earth[3].

Summary

We have seen that the sacrificial system is not a contradiction of the salvation work of Jesus, and that He did not do away with the sacrifices. As sacrifices aren't capable by themselves to take away sin, they can be performed now or in the future without blaspheming Jesus Name as the true lamb of God.

While we as Christians do not need the Temple for our personal salvation, we can see that it is part of the ultimate restoration of Israel and is preparing the way for the Messiah.

Christians have stood with Israel in the past and opened crucial doors in the restoration process. Perhaps Christians will again be used by God to open up doors for Israel – this time when it comes to the rebuilding of the Temple?

In the next chapter we are going to view the potential impact of a rebuilt temple on both Christian and Jewish theology.

[1] "West Papua Delegation Donates Gold For Holy Temple", 7 Oct 2007, https://www.israelnationalnews.com/News/News.aspx/123837 (accessed 7 Jan 2018)

See also Kobi Nahsoni's article *Papua New Guinea delegation donates gold for rebuilding Temple*, 7 Oct 2007, https://www.ynetnews.com/articles/0,7340,L-3457263,00.html (accessed 7 Jan 2018)

[2] For more details, see Daniel Lancaster's fascinating book "*What About the Sacrifices*", (Published by First Fruits of Zion, 2011)

[3] For more on this, see Appendix 2: The Millennium and Beyond

12

A Theological Earthquake

It is my firm conviction that the Third Temple will be built shortly. If the Temple is built before the rapture of the Church, how then should the Church respond? Also, how will the Third Temple impact modern Judaism?

The Impact on Christian Theology

As a result of Israel becoming a nation in 1948, many Christians woke up to the need to significantly change their theology. Those that held to the view that Church was the new Israel, and that ancient Israel would never be restored to the Land were shown to be out of touch with God's purposes and plans as stated in the Scriptures.

The rebuilding of the Temple would similarly rock Christian theology. While the Church has correctly believed that we individually are temples of the Holy Spirit, much of the Church has done away with any possible role for the Temple for believers.

It is interesting to note that this attitude seems to significantly deviate from that of Jesus and the early disciples. Jesus frequently taught in the Temple – despite the flagrantly corrupt leadership of the priests in His day.

After the death, burial and resurrection of Jesus, the disciples continued to meet in the Temple during the hour of prayer. They preached the gospel there, they healed the sick there, and they fellowshipped and prayed there. We also read of how Paul the Apostle himself was in a hurry to return to Jerusalem in time for Pentecost (Acts 20:16). Why? Because all Jewish males were required by God to come to the Temple three times a year (Deut. 16:16).

We can therefore see that the early disciples continued to go the Temple even after the death, burial and resurrection of Jesus. This despite the fact that the priests in charge of the Temple in their day, were the very ones guilty of conspiring against and murdering Jesus.

Why did the disciples continue to go to the Temple when its leadership was so corrupt? I believe the answer is simply that they honoured the holiness of the site – they believed in God's promise to King Solomon that *"My name (will) be there forever; and My eyes and My heart will be there perpetually"* and that *"My eyes will be open and My ears attentive to prayer made in this place"*.(2 Chron 7:12-16)

If they kept meeting in the Temple with such a corrupt leadership in place, shouldn't we as Christians be able to go to a future Third Temple – even if we do not agree with the teachings of some of the rabbis in charge? I believe we can on the basis of recognizing the holiness of the site in the eyes of God.

It is true that the Third Temple will one day be desecrated by the antichrist. We need to remember that this necessitates that it will in the first place be a place considered holy to God. After all, only a place that is holy to God in the first place can truly be desecrated. If God considers the place holy, then shouldn't we?

The Temple being rebuilt would truly be a great End Time sign as it would set the stage for Jesus' return. Much of the modern Church has lost its focus on the End Times, on the prophetic role of Israel and on the Lord's return. If we are still on this earth at the building of the Third Temple, it should serve as a wake-up call to the body of Christ to be prepared for the Lord's coming.

The Temple being rebuilt would force many Christians to re-evaluate their theologies, and as they do, many will come to realize the significance of this site in God's eyes. It will also force us back to a view of the Temple more closely resembling that of the early disciples and will also point us strongly to the soon coming of our Lord and Saviour.

The Impact on Modern Judaism

Orthodox Jews have prayed for the rebuilding of the Temple twice daily for the past 1900+ years. It's rebuilding will be another vivid sign to the nation of Israel that the God of Israel lives and answers prayer today!

The Temple will also help Israel understand the sacrifice of Jesus on the cross. After the destruction of the Temple in 70 AD, Rabbinic Judaism shifted away from sacrifices to instead promote good works as the means to right standing with God. This view is simply not consistent with Scripture, as *"it is the blood that makes atonement for the soul"* (Lev. 17:11).

Without animal sacrifices for over 1900 years, the concept of blood being shed for forgiveness – and ultimately the sacrificial death of Jesus - appears foreign to Rabbinic Judaism. A modern-day restoration of the Temple sacrifices would again make the death of the innocent on behalf of our sins real in the hearts and minds of the Jewish people. This could indeed be a significant step towards the day when the whole nation will look upon the one whom they pierced and mourn in repentance as they have a revelation of His sacrifice and mercy (Zec 12:10-13:1). As we pray for the Jewish nation in these End Times, may our prayers echo the words of Paul *'my heart's desire and prayer to God for Israel is that they may be saved"* (Rom 10:1)

Summary

Ultimately, the rebuilding of the Temple will challenge both Christian and Jewish theologies, bringing them both closer to their biblical roots and pointing graphically to the need for holiness in the presence of God. The rebuilding of the Temple will be a great End Time sign to the Church. It will also be part of the process of revealing to Israel and the world, the 'Lamb who was slain'.

We now move to the appendices of this book, where we will first look at a novel theory about the original Temple location, then look at the great Temple building project of the Millennium, before closing with a personal challenge from the worship of the Temple.

APPENDIXES

THE CITY OF DAVID THEORY

Was the Temple really located on the Temple Mount?

In recent years, Bob Cornuke and Dr Martin Young have proposed that the Temple was not actually located on what we today call the Temple Mount.

This theory obviously has huge implications for Bible prophecy and the rebuilding of the Temple. But does it fit the Biblical and archaeological evidence?

Dr Martin Young and Bob Cornuke's Temple Theory

In 1867, archaeologists made the stunning discovery that the original City of David was not located inside the walls of what is known as the Old City of Jerusalem, but rather to the south of and outside these walls. The conventional ideas concerning the location of ancient Jerusalem were shown to be wrong through this one significant breakthrough in archaeological research.

City of David in foreground, Temple Mount in background
Ariely (https://commons.wikimedia.org/wiki/File:City_of_David.jpg), „City of David", Added City of David Markings, https://creativecommons.org/licenses/by/3.0/legalcode

THE CITY OF DAVID THEORY

Based on this research, Dr Martin Young went even further to suggest that the Temple could not have been located on the Temple Mount, but rather in the newly rediscovered City of David to the south.

The main thrust of the theory is that:

1. The Temple needed water to rinse away the sacrifices. It therefore had to be located close to Jerusalem's only water source – the Gihon spring in the City of David – rather than at the modern 'Temple Mount'.
2. Furthermore, Dr. Young pointed to Jesus' prediction of *'not one stone shall be left here upon another'* (Matt 24:2). The massive stones left in the Western Wall appear to contradict the very words of Jesus if indeed the Temple Mount was the site.
3. Primarily based on these two main ideas, Dr Young proclaimed that the Temple must therefore have been located in the City of David and not on the Temple Mount
4. Finally, building on references from Josephus, Dr Young made the case that the massive structure today known as the 'Temple Mount' was rather the Roman Fortress of Antonia

Bob Cornuke has succeeded in popularizing Dr Young's work through his 2014 book "TEMPLE: Amazing New Discoveries That Change Everything About the Location of Solomon's Temple".

The implications of this theory when it comes to Bible Prophecy are dramatic. If this theory is true, it could open the way for the rebuilding of the Temple without sparking World War 3! In this way, it could open up the door for the Third Temple in a much simpler way than previously thought.

THE CITY OF DAVID THEORY

Looking at the Biblical and Archaeological Record

While proponents of the Cornuke and Young theory are excited about its possibilities, questions are raised from both Biblical and Archaeological perspectives.

The Scriptures are very clear that the Temple of Solomon was built on a threshing floor at Mount Moriah. 2 Chron. 3:1 tells us: *"Now Solomon began to build the house of the Lord at Jerusalem on Mount Moriah, where the Lord had appeared to his father David, at the place that David had prepared on the threshing floor of Ornan the Jebusite"* (emphasis added). So for the Cornuke theory to be true, Mount Moriah and the threshing floor must have been located in the original City of David.

UK based Bible teacher Pastor Derek Walker points out that the City of David is hardly a mountain. The city is in fact surrounded by mountains and is situated lower than the surrounding areas. It is therefore a poor fit by any measure for the Biblical 'Mount Moriah'.

The first mention of Mount Moriah in Scripture is as the mountain on which Abraham was to sacrifice Isaac. Ps Derek Walker points out that if Mount Moriah was located inside the City of David - as necessitated by this theory - then at the time of Abraham, the mountain would have been inside the city of Salem where Melchizedek was serving as priest. However, the biblical account gives no indication that the sacrifice of Isaac was taking place inside a crowded city!

Finally, Walker points out that the Temple of Solomon was built on a threshing floor on Mount Moriah. Threshing floors were places where the wheat was threshed and separated from the chaff - and the worthless chaff would then be removed. For this reason, threshing floors would often be located on higher ground outside a city to facilitate the wind gently blowing away the chaff, leaving only the precious grain behind[1].

Let's also remember that in 2 Chron. 5:2, the Ark of the covenant was taken *'out* of the City of David' to the temple built by King Solomon. In other words, the Temple was not built inside the city of David.

Another point against Cornuke's theory is the 'Stone of Trumpeting'. This stone was inscribed in clear Hebrew with the words 'to the place of trumpeting' and was found among other stones that the Romans had thrown down from what is now known as the Temple Mount to the pavement below. It is hard to see what a stone with this inscription would do in a Roman fortress as alleged by Cornuke, and makes more sense for it to have been part of the Temple.

Stone of Trumpeting - inscription in top left
Ekeidar (https://commons.wikimedia.org/wiki/File:Ancient_Jerusalem,_A_remnant_of_the_temple_walls.jpg), „Ancient Jerusalem, A remnant of the temple walls", https://creativecommons.org/licenses/by-sa/3.0/legalcode

As Jesus was gazing at the magnificent Temple buildings (Matt 24:1-2), it is true that He said: *'not one stone shall be left here upon another'*. And while the Temple buildings were destroyed as foretold, the gigantic retaining wall that upheld the huge Temple

THE CITY OF DAVID THEORY

Mount plaza remains standing to this day. A completely destroyed Temple Mount as suggested by Young & Cornuke could fit Jesus' prediction. However, the current Temple Mount with its retaining wall could also fit Jesus' Words as Jesus was specifically talking about the destruction of the buildings of the Temple Mount and not the actual retaining wall itself.

Finally, Cornuke's theory asserts that the Temple needed a source of water to wash away the sacrifices – and that since the Spring of Gihon in the City of David was Jerusalem's only source of water, the Temple would have to be located nearby. However, the Jewish records show how the Temple was supplied independently with water via an aquaduct from a spring near Bethlehem, overcoming this hindrance[4]. Furthermore, you would not place the Temple with its blood sacrifices over the city of Jerusalem's only reliable water source! The blood and guts would quickly have polluted the water leading to serious problems for the city.

As of 2022, I am unaware of any serious Jewish temple activist organization that has embraced Cornuke's theory. However, even among Jewish organisations there is a level of doubt and controversy concerning the exact location of the Temple on the Temple Mount. While excavations on the Temple Mount would quickly resolve this debate, for now we just have to watch and pray.

Let us pray for God's purposes to come to pass, for His decrees and will to be done on earth as in Heaven. God has always longed to dwell among His people, and the day is coming soon when He will indeed return and dwell among Jew and Gentile. May that day come soon and may we all be found ready at His Coming!

In the next appendix, we will look at the massive worldwide building project of the Temple during Christ's 1000 year reign – and will also look at the Temple and its place in Eternity.

[1] Walker, Derek. *The true Location of the Temple*, Jul 4, 2017: https://www.youtube.com/watch?v=yU5ozcdN1zU (accessed Jan 9, 2018). For further details see Dr David Reagan, *The Jewish Temples,* http://christinprophecy.org/articles/the-jewish-temples/

THE MILLENIUM AND BEYOND

While the First and Second Temples played key roles in ancient Israel, and while the Third Temple features in the End Times, the Bible also reveals a role for the Temple in the 1000-year reign of Christ and even in eternity.

The Millennium

Oh what a glorious day it will be! We all long for that day when Jesus returns in power and glory and defeats the anti-Christ and his wicked forces. Jesus will then usher in a reign of peace, where we will reign *'with Christ for a thousand years'* (Rev 20:4).

What will this reign look like? The Scriptures show that it will be a literal reign on earth by Jesus Himself. It was prophesied by none less than the Archangel Gabriel that Jesus would one day sit on the throne of His father David (Luke 1:32). David never reigned as king in heaven or set up his throne there – it was on earth, and specifically in Jerusalem that David ruled. For this familiar prophecy from the nativity story to be fulfilled, Jesus must at some point reign from Jerusalem in Israel. I believe the Scriptural evidence points to this happening during the Millennium.

Ezekiel chapters 38-39 describe the great End Time Gog and Magog war, ending with Israel knowing that *"that I am the Lord their God from that day forward"* (Ezek 39:22).

The next 8 chapters of Ezekiel go into detail about a massive Temple being built – assumedly after this war has ended and after Jesus' return in glory. The size of this Temple could not possibly fit on the existing Temple Mount or even within the boundaries of Jerusalem's Old City.[1] It seems that significant topical changes will make this possible. The area to the south of Jerusalem will become a plain (Zec 14:10), the Mount of Olives will be split in two (Zec 14:4) and the city itself will be rocked by a massive earthquake (Rev. 11:13).[2] The end result of this upheaval is that the *'mountain of the Lord's temple (will be) established as the highest of the mountains'*. (Isa 2:2, Mic 4:1, Ezek 40:2).

The Millennial Building Project
"Arise, shine;
For your light has come!
And the glory of the Lord is risen upon you.
For behold, the darkness shall cover the earth,
And deep darkness the people;
But the Lord will arise over you,
And His glory will be seen upon you.
The Gentiles shall come to your light,
And kings to the brightness of your rising." Is 60:1-3

While Isaiah 60 is often quoted in churches and applied in various ways, its context shows that it is primarily about the Millennial temple building project. Let's look in detail at this chapter's magnificent prophecy.

Verse 3 declares that the gentiles will be coming to 'your light' – in other words to the light that will shine on, in and through Israel. The same verse goes on to say that not only gentiles will be coming, but even 'kings to the brightness of your rising'. In addition to the Gentiles and their kings coming to Israel, verse 5 declares that 'the abundance of the sea' shall be given to Israel and that the 'wealth of the gentiles' shall come to her. While some Christians eagerly apply this verse to themselves, the context is describing the nations coming with wealth to Israel for a specific purpose explained later in the chapter.

Verse 6 goes on to describe trains of camels and dromedaries coming bearing gold and incense, while verse 7 portrays flocks and rams coming in droves to be sacrificed on the altar of God's house.

Verse 11 describes the gates of the city of Jerusalem remaining open 24/7 to accommodate the massive ongoing processions of gentile wealth and gentile kings coming to the city. Why are they all coming to town, why all these sacrifices – and why all this wealth? We see the answer in verse 13; they are all flocking to Jerusalem in order to *'beautify the place of my sanctuary'*.

This passage reminds us of the story of the Tabernacle built by Moses in the wilderness and the freewill offering that was taken from the people to build God's habitation with gold, silver and precious materials (Ex 35-36). Having experienced God's presence and heard His voice at Mt Sinai, the Israelites flocked to donate their silver and their gold – reaching the point where Moses had to start turning them away. Isaiah's account of the building of the Millennial Temple seems to tell a similar story – with the whole world participating in a massive outpouring of wealth to beautify God's House in Jerusalem.

What a change it will be in those days from business as usual. For century after century the Jews, Jerusalem and Israel have been despised and hated by the nations, and we know this hatred will only intensify in the End Times. However, there is coming a day when it will all turn around, as Isaiah says to Israel: *'all those who despised you shall fall prostrate at the soles of your feet'* (verse 14).

While the nations of the world today are keeping their embassies away from Jerusalem, in that day, top level delegations from the nations will hastily come to the King of Kings in Jerusalem. Zechariah tells us that at that time, all nations will start coming up to Jerusalem's Temple year by year to celebrate the Feast of Tabernacles (Zec 14:16-19).

May that glorious day come soon when the Lord Himself will tabernacle among His people in His Temple and all nations will know that He is God.

The Temple in Eternity

While Isaiah 60 talks about the Millennial Temple, Revelation Chapters 21 and 22 give us a glimpse of eternity. These chapters start off by describing a new heaven and a new earth, with the glorious new city of Jerusalem coming down to earth from heaven.

Interestingly, the New Jerusalem has *'no Temple... for the Lord God Almighty and the Lamb are its temple'* (Rev 21:22).

It would appear that the reason the New Jerusalem has no Temple in it, is that it is fashioned after the Holy of Holies of the Temple. Consider these parallels:

- The Holy of Holies is a perfect cube, as is the new Jerusalem
- The Holy of Holies was covered entirely in gold, while the new Jerusalem has streets of pure gold
- The Holy of Holies had no natural source of light and its only light source was God's glory itself. Likewise, the New Jerusalem needs neither sun or moon, for the 'glory of God illuminated it' (Rev 21:23)
- Nothing unclean could enter the Holy of Holies. In the same way, nothing that defiles will enter the New Jerusalem, only those whose names are in the Lamb's book of life (Rev 21:27)

It would seem then that the New Jerusalem has no temple as it is actually resembling the Holy of Holies itself! God will then dwell among His people as He has intended from the very beginning of time.

We have seen in this book how God had a purpose for the first and second Temples, that He has a plan for the third Temple, millennial Temple and the New Jerusalem. The Temple was patterned after a divine blueprint (Heb 8:5) and it should therefore not surprise us to see the key role it plays in God's past, present and future plans.

Coming back to the here and now, may we live our lives as living temples to God. May our lives be truly cleansed by the blood of the Lamb, may our hearts be set apart for worshipping Him only, and may we give the very best to Him alone. And as we do, we will find that His glory and His sweet presence will fill the temples of our hearts – for truly God's desire is to dwell right in our midst even right now.

[1] Grant, Jeffrey. *The New Temple and the Second Coming*, , page 180

[2] Glashouwer, Willem J. *Why Jerusalem*, pages 88-89

ENTERING THE HOLY OF HOLIES

We started this book by talking about how the Temple was all about God and was God-focused. Let us finish this book in a similar way by turning our focus to the worship in the Temple.

Past the Outer Court

"Take me past the outer court,
and through the holy place,
past the brazen altar,
Lord I want to see your face.....

Take me into the Holy of Holies,
take me in by the Blood of the Lamb,
Take me into the Holy of Holies,
Take the coal, cleanse my lips, here I am'

Growing up in church during a time of revival, this song quickly became one of my favourite worship songs. As the lyrics of the song filled our church, I would close my eyes and imagine passing through the outer courts of the Temple and ascending the steps to the Holy Place. From there, I would continue on until I reached the veil separating the Holy Place from the Holy of Holies and would pause before entering the presence of the Most High.

I would imagine myself in the presence of Almighty God in that sacred place and bow down before Him in worship. I would wonder what I would say to Him, would I thank Him for what He has done in my life, would I ask Him for something that was on my heart or would I simply stretch out my hands and honour the King of Kings? And what would He say to me in turn as I waited on Him in that special place?

Ultimately, the Temple is all about Him – having all these external paraphernalia without God is in and of itself meaningless. But as the Temple was filled with glory, the meaning and purpose of the Temple was revealed.

Our lives reflect the same truth. We can fill our lives with lots of activity, but it is truly only as our hearts are filled with God's presence that we find our true purpose and meaning.

The Father is looking for true worshippers, who will worship Him in Spirit and in Truth (John 4:23). May you and I truly be among those who pass through the outer court and enter in to the Holy of Holies. May we daily bow down and humble ourselves before the Almighty Creator of the Universe. And may we lift our hands in worship in thanksgiving for what He has done in our lives.

The Lord's Return

Ultimately, the Third Temple is all about preparing the way for the Messiah's return. Many churches have lost the vision of the End Times but may we truly in this hour re-capture the vision of the Lord's soon coming.

Just as the Temple Institute is preparing for the Third Temple, so let us prepare ourselves just as thoroughly for the day when the Lord will come.

I'd like to thank you for coming on this journey with me in this book. While it has contained lots of information about current events, I pray that this book will truly excite you about Jesus' soon return. As Paul said, may we truly be among those who 'look for and hasten the Lord's coming' (2 Pet 3:12).

Amen!

SELECTED BIBLIOGRAPHY

Decker, David. *Revival from Zion: Fifty Reasons Christians Should Support the Temple*, Tarshish Ltd, 2005

Fruchtenbaum, Arnold. *In The Footsteps of the Messiah*, San Antonio, Tex: Ariel Press, 2003

Jeffrey, Grant. *The New Temple and the Second Coming*, Colorado Springs, CO: Waterbook Press, 2007

Glashouwer, Willem J. *Why Jerusalem*, The Netherlands, Christians for Israel International, 2015

Lancaster, Daniel. *What About the Sacrifices?*, First Fruits of Zion, 2011

Oren, Michael B. *Six Days of War: June 1967 and the Making of the Modern Middle East*, New York: Random House Publishing, 2003

Richardson, Joel. *The Islamic Anti-Christ*, Los Angeles, CA: WND Books, 2009

Richardson, Joel. *MidEast Beast, The Scriptural Case for an Islamic Anti-Christ*, Washington DC: WND Books, 2012

Rosenberg, Joel C. *Epicenter: Why the current rumblings in the Middle East Will Change Your Future*, Carol Stream, IL: Tyndale Publishing House 2008

Enoch Lavender writes regular articles about current events as they relate to Bible Prophecy and is a regular contributor to Christian newspapers, magazines and web sites in the US, UK, Australia and New Zealand.

Enoch's teaching programs can been seen on TBN pacific and on Becoming Greater TV. In addition, Enoch hosts a popular YouTube channel with a growing international following and featuring over 100 of his teaching messages.

Enoch has been studying Hebrew and the Jewish origins of Christianity for the past 10 years and is based with his wife and three kids in Melbourne, Australia.

His latest articles, teaching videos and products are all available at www.pastorenoch.com.au

Printed in the USA
CPSIA information can be obtained
at www.ICGtesting.com
LVHW011429200324
774975LV00013B/527